Roc

Jacqueline James

Rock of my Salvation

# Rock of my Salvation

## By Jacqueline James

# TABLE OF CONTENTS
## Chapter 1. Faith

2 Corinthians 5,7 KJV
James 1,4 KJV
James 1,6 KJV
Matthew 21,21-22 KJV
Romans 10,10 KJV
Hebrews 11,6 KJV

# Chapter 2. Hope

Jeremiah 29,11 KJV
Romans 12,12 KJV
Jeremiah 17,7 KJV
Psalm 62,5-6 KJV
Isaiah 40,31 KJV

## Chapter 3. Peace...

Psalm 29,11 KJV
John 14,27 KJV
Romans 16,20 KJV
Matthew 5,9 KJV
Psalm 119,165 KJV
Galatians 5,22-23 KJV

# Chapter 4. Redemption

Galatians 2,20 KJV
Hebrews 9,15 KJV
Isaiah 44,22 KJV
2 Peter 3,9 KJV
John 3,16 KJV
John 10,10 KJV

# Chapter 5. Salvation

Philippians 2,12-13 KJV
John 14,6 KJV
Ephesians 1,13-14 KJV
1 Thessalonians 5,9-10 KJ
Acts 2,38 KJV
Acts 4,12 KJV

## About the Author

The author Jacqueline James is constantly evolving through her spiritual walk. She expresses these revolutionary progressions throughout her writing.

Jacqueline James is a published author who specializes in poetry with a great passion for children's stories. She has proven her devotion through her relentless work. Jacqueline spends hours of research in the interest of (you) the readers to develop a personal connection through each of her books. Jacqueline books explode with passion leaving (you) the readers with a great sense of fulfillment from her work. After thoroughly exploring Jacqueline poetry her intentions are to give (you) the readers an extraordinary sense of peace. Jacqueline is very appreciative that (you) the readers have chosen to follow her on this amazing journey that God has embarked upon her life.

# The Dedication

Rock of my Salvation, is dedicated to my older cousin Monica Adams,

Thank you, Monica, for your guidance during my adolescence years. Watching your resilience through life challenges helped strengthen me for the upcoming obstacles that I faced as a young adult. I was always able to reflect on your wisdom as a road map for survival. For that and many other insights that you've shared I'm forever grateful. I'm extremely honored to have you as part of my upbringing, and I will always treasure our special connection.

With love always your "baby cousin"
Jacqueline James aka "Do-Do"

# Introduction

This book "Rock of my Salvation" allows you to explore
several avenues through your spiritual walk.
The purpose is to enrich you with knowledge and
admiration for the gospel of Christianity through the art of
poetry. Within the book contents you will find scriptures
from the KJV bible, at the beginning of each chapter.
Afterwards carefully selected poetry written by the author
to support the essence of the scripture will follow. At the
end of each chapter the author offers an affirmation as a
guide to enhance your confidence through your spiritual
journey.

Relax and absorb what the author is offering to enrich you
through peace as your faith continues to grow.

# Chapter 1. Faith

2 Corinthians 5,7 KJV
James 1,4 KJV
James 1,6 KJV
Matthew 21,21-22 KJV
Romans 10,10 KJV
Hebrews 11,6 KJV

# Jacqueline James

2 Corinthians 5,7 KJV
(For we walk by faith, not by sight,)

James 1,4 KJV
But let patience have her perfect work, that ye may be
perfect and entire, wanting nothing.

James 1,6 KJV
But let him ask in faith, nothing g wavering. For he that
wavereth h is like a wave of the sea driven with the wind
and tossed.

Matthew 21,21-22 KJV
Jesus answered and said unto them, Verily I say unto you,
If ye have faith, and doubt not, ye shall not only do this
which is done to the fig tree, but also if ye shall say unto
this mountain, Be thou removed, and be thou cast into the
sea, it shall be done. [22] And all things, whatsoever ye
shall ask in prayer, believing, ye shall receive.

Romans 10,10 KJV
For with the heart man believeth unto righteousness, and
with the mouth confession is made unto salvation.

Hebrews 11,6 KJV
But without faith it is impossible to please him for he that
cometh to God must believe that he is, and that he is a
rewarder of them that diligently seek him

# Rock of my Salvation...

God is the rock of my salvation,
I trust Him with all of my heart and soul for His protection,

If I fall, He's forever there to catch me,
Then bring my spirit to my place of peace,

I never once had to second guess or think twice,
God's word is where I receive my trusted advice,

I seek God through prayer for my refuge,
He then cast my burdens to complete relief,

God delivers me from trouble and brings me out,
Through my Savior's words there's never a doubt,

God is the perfect rock that guides my life,
He rewards my days and blesses my nights,

When I submit to His will God takes control,
God forgives my sin then saves my soul.

God is the rock of my salvation,
Jesus is His perfect living creation!

Jacqueline James

# *Faith...*

Faith is when we put something into the atmosphere,
Then walk into it without doubt or fear,

Once we trust in God to deliver us through,
Afterwards we're more than a conqueror when He's
through,

Faith is not only what we believe,
It's also what has been dropped into our spirit to receive,

God is moved by our faith,
The very substance is what He contemplates,

When we feed our faith by starving our doubt,
God's blessing will continue to reign throughout,

From faith to faith is when we knew God blessed our past,
Then we trust that our future blessings will also surpass.

# Lord I'm Thankful...

Lord I'm thankful for all that You've done,
You save my soul by sending Your only begotten son,

Lord I'm thankful for You and all that You do,
You extend Your grace as I go through,

Lord I'm thankful for the air that I breathe,
You show me mercy and for that I'm pleased,

Lord I'm thankful for the life You gave,
You bring me new hope each time I pray,

Lord I'm thankful for Your perfect peace,
With my faith in You it shall not cease,

Lord I'm thankful for Jesus as my friend,
His precious blood washed away my sins,

Jacqueline James


Lord I'm thankful for things that I don't understand,
I surrender my 'will' to Your command,


Lord I'm thankful for all of my days,
I give You the glory with my praise.

# Spiritual Eye...

I see things through my spiritual eye,
Sometimes I see things as they are happening,
Sometimes I see things once they have happened,

I don't control what the spirit allows me to see,
I only accept the gift as it is given to me,

God sends me visions through my spirit,
I open up my heart in order to hear them,

This is a true blessing over my life,
In order to ease the tension as I fight,

God has placed clear visions as my guide,
To serve as a blessing through my spiritual eye,

Jacqueline James

## *Yes, Thank You Jesus...*

Yes, thank you Jesus,
Yes, thank you Jesus,

Yes, thank you Jesus for sparing my life,
Keeping me strong enough to go through life's fight,

Yes, thank you Jesus for healing my body,
Restoring my health to testify to somebody,

Yes, thank You Jesus for my right state of mind,
For in my soul Your peace I may find,

Yes, thank You Jesus for taking control,
Over my life for which You own,

Yes, thank You Jesus for humbling my heart,
Keeping me worthy as I do my part,

Yes, thank You Jesus for Your precious blood,
Covering me with Your unconditional love,

# Rock of my Salvation

Yes, thank You Jesus for Your forgiveness,
May I honor Your word through my righteousness,

Yes, thank you Jesus for giving me another day,
That I may glorify You, this I pray.

Jacqueline James

# *Blesseth be the Virtuous Women...*

A virtuous woman above them all,
God will bless her life with His call,

Through her humility she will know,
That God is with her wherever she goes,

When her mind and heart is clear,
There's room for God's love in store for her,

God's word in her heart shall never desert,
Through her faith she'll know her worth,

The virtuous woman is busy all day,
Doing her chores as she prays,

During the night when you rest,
She's up honoring our Father as she's being blessed,

When her days and struggles become hard,
God's grace and mercy is her reward,

Blesseth be the virtuous woman,
The presence of peace with her is coming.

## Questions...

When people came to question me, about my success
through Gods ability,
God came to bless my day, from my faith, and my serenity,


They all wanted to doubt the things, I was capable of,
But God, show them all, that I was worthy of Jesus love,


He allowed my voice, to be heard around the entire world,
And those who heard, humble themselves, like that of a
little 'boy or girl!'


God messages was sent through me, in order to receive his
people, praise,
He wants to deliver them, and bless them, throughout their
days,


God also wants to help his peoples, and to save their souls,
So, he blessed me to delivery his message, and through His
words, I uphold


So, when they come with questions, my answers are always

Jacqueline James


the same,
God blessed me with a gift of poetry, to read in Jesus'
name.

# Sanctified City Girl...

The sanctified city girl,
Ruling the streets, was her world,

God stepped in, that's when her troubles end,
And, her new life began,

Jesus saved her and filled her with the grace of God,
When she humbled herself as a child,

She was transformed to a new creature through her soul,
After she relinquish to God all of her control,

Those around, that knew her name,
Saw her spirit, devoutly changed,

However, some tried to put her faith to a test,
But, because of her obedience, she was blessed,

God granted her mercy, through His grace,
So when her journey's over, she'll see His face,

Jacqueline James

# Early Bird Christian...

Early bird Christian come out and shine,
Are you ready for a spiritual rhyme?

Today's rhyme consists of love,
From our heavenly Father above,

Blessed me Father for You are my friend,
Forgive me now for I have sinned,

Some of Your rules I have misplaced,
But never have I fallen from Your grace,

Know me Father for I am yours,
Shower me with Your unconditional love,

Love me Father for I make mistakes,
Forgive me Father for Your name's sake,

Guide me Father help me through,
Teach me the righteous things to do,

Help me Lord with Your loving hands,
Change my heart on Your commands,

# Rock of my Salvation

Tame my tongue Lord as I speak,
Humble my words to the people I greet,

Keep me calm Lord humble my heart,
Bless my life Father as I do my part,

Keep my mind Lord stayed on You,
When my load is heavy Lord carry me through,

Show me mercy Lord with Your grace,
Bless my journey to see Your face,

Through my faith Lord bless my days,
To honor You always this I pray.

Jacqueline James

# God's Reason...

Through my faith God allows me to achieve,
God blesses me with a gift of hope to receive,

I tried to convince others to believe,
However, many ears were closed from selfish greed,

God places good people in my path,
Just to bear witness on His behalf,

We share testimony of our stories,
The entire while we give God His glory,

God has filled me with His loving words,
Unlike anything the world has ever heard,

God will bless you with the gift of serenity,
Allowing you to serve a multitude of many,

Your loyalty and faith will keep you strong,
Through God's words you're not alone,

You will cross many believers' paths during this season,
Not by chance, but for God's reason,

## Rock of my Salvation

Humility will set in, as you unfold,
Allowing God to step in and take control,

All of God's children's will be on one accord,
Helping others as they serve the Lord.

Jacqueline James

"Today's Affirmation"

Today I am prayerful, I am positive through my actions,
and I am powerful.
I am at peace with myself. My faith allows me to
accomplish everything through God in which I trust. I will
utilize my knowledge and resources to make the best of my
situation. I will trust in God to guide my thoughts through
each of my endeavors. My serenity will give me complete
confidence in all of my affairs.

I am prayerful,
I am positive,
I am peaceful,
I am powerful,

# Chapter 2. Hope

**Jeremiah 29,11 KJV**
**Romans 12,12 KJV**
**Jeremiah 17,7 KJV**
**Psalm 62,5-6 KJV**
**Isaiah 40,31 KJV**

1. Speak Through me Lord...
2. Deep in my Soul...
3. Nobody but Jesus...
4. How Grateful am I...
5. Humbly Blessed...
6. Dance in my Feet...
7. Be my Village...
8. 5th Prayer...
9. Go to the Land of God's Supplies...
10. Mercy and Blessings...

Jacqueline James

Jeremiah 29,11 KJV
For I know the thoughts that I think toward you, saith the Lord, thoughts of peace, and not of evil, to give you an expected end.

Romans 12,12 KJV
Rejoicing in hope, patient in tribulation, continuing instant in prayer,

Jeremiah 17,7 KJV
Blessed is the man that trusteth in the LORD, and whose hope the LORD is.

Psalm 62,5-6 KJV
My soul waits thou only upon God, for my expectation h is from him. [6] He only is my rock and my salvation, he is my defense, I shall not be moved.

Isaiah 40,31 KJV
But they that wait upon the Lord shall renew their strength, they shall mount up with wings as eagles, they shall run, and not be weary, and they shall walk, and not faint.

# Speak through Me Lord...

Lord may it be through my tongue You speak,
May the words strengthen those who are lost or weak,

May hope comes from the messages that they hear,
To deliver them from all their doubts and fear,

May they find in their hearts Your perfect peace,
To comfort their souls as their faith increase,

Lord may the words resonate in their mind,
Where Your mercy and grace they shall find,

Allow their darkest hours to be transformed into light,
As Your words bring reassurance to their lives,

Lord speak Your words of righteousness through me,
To deliver Your people a message to set their souls free.

Jacqueline James

# Deep in My Soul...

Way down deep in my soul,
I'm going to give it to Jesus, for His control,

Way down deep in my soul,
God pulled out a miracle, too much to hold,

I'm reaching in my soul, way down deep,
And, I'm pulling out blessings for God to meet,

I'm reaching way down in my soul deep,
And I'm pulling out gifts to place at my Lord's feet,

Deep, deep, deep, deep in my soul,
Where things are left in God's control,

Deep, deep, deep, deep in my soul,
For all the blessings I have to hold,

In my soul way down deep, I pray to God my soul to keep,
In my soul way down deep, I pray to God as I weep,

In my soul, in my soul, I pray to God to take control,
In my soul, in my soul, I pray to God to behold,

I can have, and I can behold,
Because I serve a master with all the control,

# Rock of my Salvation

Way down deep, deep in my soul,
Deep, deep, deep, deep in my soul,

God is my master, He's in control,
Way down deep in my soul,

I gave it to Jesus, and He took control,
Way down deep, deep in my soul,

My cup ran over with blessings, I could not hold,
Deep, deep, deep, deep in my soul,
God brought out a miracle for me to behold.

Jacqueline James

# *Nobody But Jesus...*

Nobody does it like Jesus,
Can't nobody do, me like Jesus,

He was born for that very reason,
He died, yet He lives through every season,

He overwhelms me with His peace,
And the joy I feel continues to increase,

He brings me calm, in the midst of my storm,
That reassures me, I'm in my 'Father's' arms,

All His love continues to flutter through my mind,
If you take a look, you'll find nothing but joy inside,

Can't nobody do me like Jesus He's my friend,
Nobody does it like Jesus, He washes away my sins,

He left me fresh as white the driven snow,
So, His Holy Ghost in me can flow,

People all around will hear my voice, and know,
Because, of God's mercy, I don't have to cry no more,

He filled me up, and my cup runneth over,
I am blessed, and with His blood- I am covered,

# Rock of my Salvation

Nobody does it like Jesus, how He watches me through the
night,
Can't nobody do me like Jesus, letting me shine my
'Father's' light,

He keeps my spirit raging, with the sparkles from His glow,
I'm in His perfect peace, and the world just needs to know,

He keeps my mind stayed on Him, that's the love we share
together,
I am blessed because of it, and His joy I'll feel forever,

Nobody does it like Jesus, He's my rock,
Can't nobody do me like Jesus, and that I'll never doubt!

Jacqueline James

# How Grateful Am I...

Grateful, grateful, grateful,
How grateful am I,
Today God spared my life when He heard my cry,

He took my sins and washed them away,
Cleansing my soul with brighter days,

How grateful am I,
Today God kept me clothed in my right state of mind,
He filled me with His words to keep me wise,

How grateful am I,
Today I asked God for forgiveness when I repent,
God blessed me with my health and strength,

How grateful am I,
Today God gave me another chance,
To get my house in order through His command,


How grateful am I,
God intervenes on my behalf,
He places people of good spirits in my path,

# Rock of my Salvation

How grateful am I,
God humble my soul through life's fight,
He keeps me worthy to see His light,

How grateful am I,
God chose me for His words to flow,
To honor His name as my faith shall grow.

Jacqueline James

# Humbly Blessed...

Humble yourself and receive God's blessing,
Go through life fight, to receive God's lesson,

Surrender yourself, and receive God's grace,
Obey Gods word, and see Gods face,

Cleanse yourself and your sin will decrease,
Summit to His will, and you'll find Gods peace,

Devote yourself, and you'll find God's loyal,
Have faith, and you'll sit amongst His royal,

Have patience, and He'll give you purpose,
Call on his 'name', and He'll answer for certain,

Pray to him, and He'll hear your cry,
Lift Him in praise, and He'll be with you, bye, and bye.

# Dance in my Feet...

Please Lord keep the dance in my feet,
As I honor You Father keep Your praise in my speech,

Allow me God to testify to the people I meet,
About Your perfect peace in my life that I seek,

Lord help Your humility stay on my tongue,
Even when my road is long and my days are hard,

Lord show, me a pathway when the clouds hang low,
Cover me with grace as Your spirit through me flow,

Forgive my sins Lord as I call Your name,
Purge my heart so it doesn't remain the same,

Lord show, me mercy as You transform my ways,
Bless me Father through my faith I pray.

Jacqueline James

# Be My Village...

Be my village guide me with advice,
Help me along the way to understand my life,

Be my confidant in my time of need,
Help me to understand that life isn't free,

Help me carry my heavy loads,
Lighten my burdens as they unfold,

Support my daily needs along my path,
Intervene with love on my behalf,

Go with me Lord on every quest,
It's Your loyalty that I request,

Be my entire village on my journey,
With Your presence I have no worries.

# 5th Prayer...

I spend the New Year's Eve on my knees,
Praying to God to help me please,

I thank you Lord, for all the things You've done,
When You sent Your only begotten son,

You covered me with Your precious blood,
And, showed me mercy, through Your love,

You brought me through my darkest hour,
And, blessed me to receive Your Holy Ghost Power,

You forgave me over, and over again, for my sins,
When I allowed You to be my closest friend,

You helped me to keep my mind on You,
And, showed me the righteous things to do,

You humbled my spirit more each day,
And, saved my soul as I prayed,

You gave me Your amazing grace,
And, prepared me for the day, to see Your face.

Jacqueline James

# Go to the Land of God's Supplies...

Go from the land of not enough,
To the land of just enough,
Trust in God's plan when things get tough,

There's a land of even,
There's a land of strategy for each season,
God puts blessings in place for that reason,

Go from the land of just enough,
To the land of more than enough,
God will grant you more to share with others whose lives
are rough,

Go to the land of God's plenty of,
That will supply you with all of God's unconditional love.

# Mercy & Blessing...

In order to receive God's unconditional blessings,
We must all deal with our own indiscretions,

If you want to hear the voice of the Lord,
Then you must avoid the unnecessary noise,

When you stop allowing others to control your thoughts,
God's instructions will bring your potentials out,

God gives mercy to those who believe,
Through faithful prayer they shall receive,

Whenever you trust and work hard for the Lord,
Then you shall reap all of His goodness as your reward,

Once we submit to God's word through the challenges we
face,
God will grant us mercy through His amazing grace.

Jacqueline James

"Today's Affirmation"

Today I am hopeful in purist of my accomplishments. I am
confident through God's direction that I will successfully
achieve my goals. I am more than a conqueror of my
destiny through Christ Jesus who strengthens me.

God gives me the insurance to move forward with my
mission. I have been fully blessed by His permission.

I am hopeful
I am confident
I am a conqueror
I am blessed

# Chapter 3. Peace...

**Psalm 29,11 KJV**
**John 14,27 KJV**
**Romans 16,20 KJV**
**Matthew 5,9 KJV**
**Psalm 119,165 KJV**
**Galatians 5,22-23 KJV**

1. Stand up for God...
2. God's Favor...
3. Laid Back...
4. Your Love for me Lord...
5. Lord You Touched me...
6. I'm Sanctified...
7. Humble Yourself...
8. Rise Above...
9. I Serve to Serve...
10. Shattered Souls...

Psalm 29,11 KJV
The Lord will give strength unto his people, the Lord will bless his people with peace.

John 14,27 KJV
Peace I leave with you, my peace I give unto you, not as the world giveth, give I unto you. Let not your heart be troubled, neither let it be afraid.

Romans 16,20 KJV
And the God of peace shall bruise Satan under your feet shortly. The grace of our Lord Jesus Christ be with you. Amen.

Matthew 5,9 KJV
Blessed are the peacemakers, for they shall be called the children of God.

Psalm 119,165 KJV
Great peace have they which love thy law, and nothing shall offend them.

Galatians 5,22-23 KJV
But the fruit of the Spirit is love, joy, peace, longsuffering, gentleness, goodness, faith, [23] Meekness, temperance, against such there is no law.

# *Stand up for God...*

Get up people and take your rightful seat,
Our Lord and Savior is building up the strong and uplifting
the weak,

God wants us to prosper in every way that we can,
By utilizing our resources and keeping His commands,

God has plans for us to follow with specific purpose,
That's designed to help us and render His people services,

We are all meant to serve Him on one accord,
Whenever we help each other, God blesses us with great
reward,

Whenever you find life difficult and feel as if you're falling,
God's mercy will help each of you act, in your true calling,

He strengthens us during our struggling times,
When prayer and praise stay on our minds,

Once we put our trust in God to take control,
Then His perfect "will " in our lives will start to unfold,

If we give God the glory throughout our lives,
He will lighten our burdens during life fight,

Jacqueline James

God will keep us encouraged as we go through,
Then we become more than conquerors when He gets
through.

# God's Favor...

My favorite favor from the Lord,
Is when He blesses my life with great joy,

God grants me mercy throughout my days,
Then He shows me favor along the way,

He gives me shelter in the midst of my storm,
While cradling me safely in the comfort of His arms,

God restores my faith to be complete,
Then pours His blessing from my head to my feet,

God soothes my challenges throughout my path,
When there's trouble, He intervenes on my behalf,

He keeps a light shining on me,
With infinite amounts of possibilities,

I'm truly grateful for all God does,
As He covers my life with His endless love.

Jacqueline James

# *Laid Back...*

Laid back, preaching God's good news,
Praying for all the empty souls, that's out there confused,

With my mind on my bible, and my bible on my mind,
It's in God's Holy word, where peace I find,

Laid back learning a spiritual lesson,
Waiting on God to bring me my blessings,

With my mind on my bible, and my bible on my mind,
I'm following my Jesus, who's one of a kind,

Laid back trap in His thoughts,
Thanking my Lord, for bringing me out,

Laid back praising His name,
Because, of His mercy, I'll never be the same,

# Rock of my Salvation

Laid back with my mind on my bible, and my bible on my
mind,
With my little light, I'm going to let it shine,

Laid back worshipping my Father throughout my days,
Loving my Lord, more and more, as I praise,

Laid back with my mind on my bible, and my bible on my
mind,
When God calls for a 'good and faithful servant', then it's
my time.

Jacqueline James

# Your Love for me Lord...

Lord when the night falls and I lose my way,
Draw me close to You Lord as I pray,

From my desperate need Lord hear my cry,
Keep my tongue worthy from morning till nigh,

Lord give an ear to hear my Master's call,
A heart to receive Your love above them all,

Show me mercy Lord over my life,
Lighten my load as I fight,

Lord humble me gently through all You do,
Keep my heart desires stayed on You,

Lord grace me with Your presence of love,
Then prepare my spirit for my Father above.

# *Lord You Touched Me...*

Lord You touched me, when no one else was there,
I was overwhelmed by Your presence, because you care,

You gave me strength preceding everything,
You are my Savior and my King,

Lord you blessed me over and over again,
You are my deliverer and my friend,

Lord you healed me on my sick bed,
You kept your 'word', on every promise, You've made,

Lord You gave me hope when all hope, was lost,
When You sent Your only begotten son to die upon the
cross,

Lord You forgave me for all of my sins,
After I repented, and allowed You, to come in,

Jacqueline James

Lord You made a way for me when there wasn't a way,
Because of it, I'm grateful each and every day,

Lord You opened doors for me to walk through,
Each step I made brought me closer to You.

# I'm Sanctified...

I am sanctified, set aside for the Master's use,
I am chosen from many, of a few,


He uses me in a way, you will never understand,
I'm here to deliver His truth, to every woman and man,


I'm here to tell His people, about His kingdom,
So they'll prepare themselves, for the glory He'll bring
them,


I'm not claiming to be a prophet, I'm just a messenger,
To grace the world, with some of God's blessings,


I try to live righteously; however, I often fall,
So I give it to God in prayer, and Jesus name I call,


He's a merciful God, so He forgives me every time,
He's my Lord and Savior, and the only one of His kind,

Jacqueline James

He's the Alpha, and the Omega, the beginning, and the end,
I'm very honored, to have Him as my friend,


I'll serve Him faithfully, with my dying breath,
I must share His greatness, I can't keep it to myself,
I enjoy being sanctified, being set aside,
For the Master's use, for Jesus to come inside,

# Humble Yourself...

Humble yourself and be kind to others,
Respect yourself, your father, and your mother,

Live every day as if it's your last day,
Allow Jesus in your heart as you humbly pray,

Praise God's name as you lift your voice,
Pray without cease throughout its course,

Give God the glory for your daily work,
Then in your life His shall not desert,

Be slow to angry, yet quick to repent,
Jesus blood was shed so forgiveness you'll get,

Forgive others that may have offended you,
Because of God's mercy it's the right thing to do,


Don't harper thoughts over any ill feelings,
Because we serve a God that always in the blessing
business,

Jacqueline James

Be a faithful servant to all those around,
God will brighten your days with cheerful smiles,

Throughout your life embrace God's amazing grace,
Then you'll spend your eternity in His sacred place.

# Rise Above...

We must continue to pray on our knees,
For God to raise us above, the world's lust and greed,

We must pray, and forgive others treacherous sins,
Then, trust in Jesus, as our closest friend,

We must ignore the blasphemy coming from them,
So, we can keep our minds, stayed on Him,

Pray to escape from their brutally,
Because, they'll never respect equality,

We must resist their evil, without temptation,
Embrace God's word, for our salvation,

Then, hide God's word in our heart,
Allow Him to take control, as we do our part,

After we've severed all their wicked tides,
God's grace will be our ultimate prize.

Jacqueline James

# 1 Serve to Serve...

I Serve to Serve,
God humbles my spirit to help those in need,
Once they are blessed then He is pleased,

As I serve others I serve the Lord,
When tasks are difficult greater are my reward,

God enriches my life each day I live,
The more that I receive the more I give,

God brings good character to my day,
When I pray for Him to have His way,

Whatever I receive from God is what I deserve,
As I serve, I serve!

# Shattered Souls...

Shattered Souls…
Shattered souls who cannot bear the heavy loads,
From the rich, the poor, the young to the old,

As their troubles in life starts to unfold,
God preserves them as He takes control,

Shattered souls who have lost their way,
Jesus will restore them all once they pray,

Shattered souls blown in the wind,
Open your hearts to allow Jesus in,

Shattered souls from evil thoughts that have been sent,
God will mend your heart together again, once you repent,

Shattered souls who have desperate needs,
God's word is the answer for them to received,

Shattered souls who are lacking in their faith,
Jesus' unconditional love will help them to embrace,

Jacqueline James

Shattered souls who have had many doubts,
Once they put their trust in God's they won't go without,

Shattered souls have now found their way,
God spared their lives because they prayed.

# Rock of my Salvation

"Today's Affirmation"

Today I have the perfect peace of Jesus in my heart. I have surrendered to God's will then He blessed my life exceedingly. I am an ordinary person doing extraordinary things.
I have courage that extends beyond my circumstances. I have a comprehensive that excels above my understanding. I am more than capable of achieving everything that my heart desires.

I am peaceful
I am prayerful
I am successful
I am complete

Jacqueline James

# Chapter 4. Redemption

**Galatians 2,20 KJV**
**Hebrews 9,15 KJV**
**Isaiah 44,22 KJV**
**2 Peter 3,9 KJV**
**John 3,16 KJV**
**John 10,10 KJV**

1. Walk with me Lord Again…
2. Thank You, Thank You Jesus…
3. God's Miracles…
4. God's Reflection…
5. God took a Break…
6. Prayer/ Patience/ Praise…
7. Walk His Talk…
8. Good Health is God's Wealth…
9. The Church…
10. God Gives…

Jacqueline James

Galatians 2,20 KJV
I am crucified with Christ, nevertheless I live, yet not I, but
Christ liveth in me, and the life which I now live in the
flesh I live by the faith of the Son of God, who loved me,
and gave himself for me.

Hebrews 9,15 KJV
And for this cause he is the mediator of the new testament,
that by means of death, for the redemption of the
transgressions that were under the first testament, they
which are called might receive the promise of eternal
inheritance.

Isaiah 44,22 KJV
I have blotted out, as a thick cloud, thy transgressions, and,
as a cloud, thy sins, return unto me, for I have redeemed
thee.

2 Peter 3,9 KJV
The Lord is not slack concerning his promise, as some men
count slackness, but is longsuffering to us-ward, not willing
that any should perish, but that all should come to
repentance.

John 3,16 KJV
For God so loved the world, that he gave his only begotten
Son, that whosoever believeth in him should not perish, but
have everlasting life.

John 10,10 KJV
The thief cometh not, but for to steal, and to kill, and to destroy, I am come that they might have life, and that they might have it more abundantly.

Jacqueline James

# Walk with me Lord Again...

Walk with me Lord,

When my load is heavy lift my feet,
Keep me worthy as I speak,

Help my mind stay on You,
Keep me safe as I go through,

Forgive me Lord from all my sins,
Walk with me through life as my best friend,

Hold me up Lord in my storm,
With You by my side no weapon shall form,


Send Your peace Lord to my heart,
Give me patience as I do my part,

Guide my steps Lord where they need to be,
Keep Your grace and mercy covering me.

# *Thank You...Thank You Jesus...*

Thank you, Jesus, for allowing me to come out of self,
To help someone else,

Thank you, Jesus, for giving me Your words to pray,
To help bless someone in their day,

Thank You Jesus for giving me strength to serve,
To help Your people with Your mercy they deserve,

Thank You Jesus for removing me from the equation,
While You bless others through me for the occasion,

Thank you, Jesus, for granting me with Your perfect peace,
That I may witness to Your people as their faith in You
increases,

Thank You Jesus for keeping me content,
Through You grace I'm free each day of my life to repent,

Thank You Jesus for blessing me with discernment,
That I may shower Your people with encouragement,

Thank You Jesus for keeping my mind stayed on You,
As You guide me through the mountains to glorify You,

Jacqueline James


Thank You for the one tongue that I have to praise Your
name,
That Your righteousness over my life shall continue to
reign.

# God's Miracles...

You are one of God's many miracles created for the world
to see,
Through His merciful love He died to set your soul free,

God gave you life, created in His image,
Blessed are you to have His spirit,

Through His spirit He graces your life,
With His unconditional love to ease your fight,

With His mercy through His grace,
He keeps you humble as you praise,

Through life challenges along the way,
You're given God's mercy each of your days.

You are one of God's miracles blessed by your life,
Your faith in Jesus will helps you to survive.

Jacqueline James

# God's Reflection...

When you do things with great selection,
It shows the beauty of God's reflection,

God's reflection will come shining through,
When you put Him in the middle of whatever you do,

Your day will be better as well as your night,
When you surround yourself by God's perfect light,

Whenever you greet people to form a connection,
Then the reflection of God will guide your actions,

God's reflection will show through others you meet,
He's beauty will flow to make things complete,

Your journey will lead you in a prosperous direction,
When your life has been blessed by God's reflection,

# God Took a Break...

God was forced to go on break in the middle of my design,
He had to regroup with my beauty on His mind,

He wanted me to be a perfect reflection of His love,
So that my heart would know how to honor my Father up
above,

His intention was for me to praise Him on command,
To accept His 'will' in my life as He blesses my land,

He designed my mind to stay on Him at all time,
To give Him the glory for the hope that I find,

He created me to always feel His perfect peace,
Each day He reassured be my faith would increase,

He designed me with compassion for His people,
Then He gifted me with humility to worship in His steeple,

He equipped me through the struggles in my life fight,
He then conditioned my soul to receive my eternal life,

## Jacqueline James

He poured in me an abundance of necessary life lessons,
Filled with beautiful rewards enriched by life blessings,


I made God sweat after He created me,
He had to write several detours before He finalized my
destiny,

# *Prayer/ Patience/ Praise...*

Prayer changes situations to your favor,
God will grant you mercy for your labor,

Patience helps you to remain humble,
God will ease your heart from life troubles,

Praise shows gratitude for all of your blessings,
God will accept your submission through life lessons,

Prayer makes the impossible possible,
God's unchanging hand is unstoppable,

Patience soothes the spirit of those who wait,
God's word will help you to keep your faith,

Praise gives you grace to honor your King,
God's loves give your heart a voice to sing,

Prayer moves the mountains from your path,
God will send others to intervene on your behalf,

Jacqueline James

Patience help to keep you focused through unsure times,
God grants you mercy when you keep Him on your mind,

Praise sends our love directly up to the Lord,
God blesses our days so that our life isn't hard.

# Walk-His-Talk...

In order for me to hear my God talk,
I had go for a total solitude walk,

I walked into my destiny by submission through faith,
In order for God to fulfill my vision I had to be patient and
wait,

It took me to control myself and tame my tongue,
And give up some worldly things that I called fun,

I made the sacrifice while God planted the seed,
Then I watered it every day through my good deeds,

I nurtured it by being obedient to His word,
Then it manifested to life after God's voice was heard,

I learnt about God's grace through an expected end,
With His mercy over my life, I expect to win,

Now I'm living through my personal testimony,
Giving God His glory with the greatest of honor.

Jacqueline James

# Good Health is God's Wealth...

God wants us to live a long and healthy life,
Filled with inspiration and love throughout our fight,

God didn't intend for us to be plague by sickness,
He wants to bless us with good health to enjoy our riches,

As we work for profits, for prosperity we praise,
Which enriches our lives for healthier days

Ecclesiastes 2,24 KJV
There is nothing better for a man, than that he should eat
and drink, and that he should make his soul enjoy good in
his labour. This also I saw that it was from the hand of
God.

Eating fruits and vegetables grown from God's land,
Along with meats for protein enhances His perfect plan,

A daily routine is what we all need,
Along with exercise to assure that we succeed,

When we participate in physical things of our choice,
This will help us to sustain a healthy heart,

# Rock of my Salvation

Our bodies are our temples that we must continuously
protect,
By educating our minds with some nutritional facts,

If by chance our bodies do become sick,
By faith God will grant us some relief quick,

Proverbs 3,7-8 KJV
Do not be wise in your own eyes, fear the Lord and shun
evil. This will bring health to your body and nourishment to
your bones.

Trust that God will not forsake you, nor leave you alone,
By His stripes we are healed, therefore we shall sing a
victorious song!

Jacqueline James

# The Church...

It's not which church that you go to,
Or, the preacher that tells you what to do,

It's how you feel when you get there,
Your spirit knows when others care,

The church is not a building,
To me is a divine Christian feeling,

With God's supernatural healing,
That brings peace to each of my dealings,

Is the satisfaction in my heart,
When God sees me during my part,

He'll know when I've done my best,
Then He'll relieve me from live stress,

He'll satisfy all of my needs,
When I pray to Him for relief,

God's Holy words I'll be learning,
As, I carry His church with me, on my journey,

# God Gives...

God Gives,
God won't give you the wind, but he'll give you His breeze,
God won't give you the land, but He will give you the trees,

God won't give you the sun, but He will give you it's
warmth,
God won't give you the seasons, but He will give you each
month,

God won't give you the ocean nor will He give you the sea,
But He will give you the oxygen from their water to breath,

God won't give you His moon that shine throughout the
night,
But He will give you its vision to help protect you by its
light,


God will give you the promises that comes in His days,
He will give each minute to take the time out to pray,

God will give you mercy and show you favor,
He will give you great reward by the fruit of your labor,

God will give you strength when you're tired and weak,
You will inherit His kingdom if you're humble and meek.

Jacqueline James


God will give you eternal life when you hide His word in
your heart,
You will receive infinite blessings when you do your part.

"Today's Affirmation"

Today I forgive others who have offended me. I forgive myself as I allow myself to be happy. I ask God for His forgiveness and I trust that He has given it. I move forward with the hope of God's glory. I trust that God has granted me His redemption. I believe that my final destiny will resolve with God eternally.
I believe that nothing in this world will hinder my purpose that God has ordained for me.

I am Humble
I am Forgiving
I am Faithful
I am Resilient

Jacqueline James

# Chapter 5. Salvation

**Philippians 2,12-13 KJV**
**John 14,6 KJV**
**Ephesians 1,13-14 KJV**
**1 Thessalonians 5,9-10 KJV**
**Acts 2,38 KJV**
**Acts 4,12 KJV**

1. God's Forgiveness...
2. God is Working on me...
3. I found God in me...
4. Global Warming or God's Warning...
5. If God taps you on the Shoulder...He shouldn't have to hit you in the...
6. Trust Him...Trust Him...Trust Him...
7. Jesus Fight my Battles...
8. Loving God's Children...
9. What did God Give Us?...
10. Gods Blessings will Shine...

Philippians 2,12-13 KJV
Wherefore, my beloved, as ye have always obeyed, not as
in my presence only, but now much more in my absence,
work out your own salvation with fear and trembling. [13]
For it is God which worketh in you both to will and to do of
his good pleasure.

John 14,6 KJV
Jesus saith unto him, I am the way, the truth, and the life,
no man cometh unto the Father, but by me.

Ephesians 1,13-14 KJV
In whom ye also trusted, after that ye heard the word of
truth, the gospel of your salvation, in whom also after that
ye believed, ye were sealed with that holy Spirit of
promise, [14] Which is the earnest of our inheritance until
the redemption of the purchased possession, unto the praise
of his glory.

1 Thessalonians 5,9-10 KJV
For God hath not appointed us to wrath, but to obtain
salvation by our Lord Jesus Christ, [10] Who died for us,
that, whether we wake or sleep, we should live together
with him.

Acts 2,38 KJV
Then Peter said unto them, Repent, and be baptized every one of you in the name of Jesus Christ for the remission of sins, and ye shall receive the gift of the Holy Ghost.

Acts 4,12 KJV
Neither is there salvation in any other, for there is none other name under heaven given among men, whereby we must be saved.

Jacqueline James

# God's Forgiveness...

God forgave us in advance for our indiscretions,
He sent His only begotten son Jesus to die for our
transgressions,

God knew that we would make mistakes,
However, we will be forgiven when we ask in His name
sake,

It doesn't matter if we know right from wrong,
We do our best when Jesus name is called,

We might offend each other in various ways,
But God offer forgiveness throughout our days,

God gives us new challenges along our journey,
Then He offers His mercy so that we don't worry,

Whenever we forgive each other, then we are also forgiven,
This is because of God's grace that we were given.

# God is Working on Me...

Regardless of how much I make or what I do,
I won't rest until God is through,

God is working on a better me,
New and improved for my soul to be free,
God is working on my redemption,
While I'm fasting praying for repentance,

God is changing my daily thoughts,
He's relieving me from demonic spirits while He cast them
out,

God is working on making me whole,
Then I'll be ready for the Master's control,

God is instilling His "will" in my life,
As I give Him the glory throughout my fight,

God is working on me,
With my acceptance it will become complete.

Jacqueline James

# I Found God in Me...

I found God,
When God found His lost sheep in me,

I found God in me,
When I learned how to live with humility,

I found God,
When I decided to embrace the gift of life,
And sincerely accepted all of life's fight,

I found God in me,
After I pushed passed my struggles and my pain,
I was able to call on His name,

I found God,
When I received His good and perfect peace,
My faith in Him instantly increased,

I found God in me,
When I put my trust in Him completely,
Afterwards my blessing came abundantly,

I found God,
When I allowed Him to take control,
His "will" in my soul forever beholds,

## Rock of my Salvation

I found in me,
When I was about my Father's business,
For serving Him has become my every decision.

Jacqueline James

# Global Warming or God's Warning...

Global warming,
With a sudden change in the temperature,
The weather that goes against the perfect order of the
atmosphere,

This is astonishing to all living creatures of nature,
Dropping snowfall during the warm months of the year,

Even the areas that never once gotten cold,
Now possess a ground covered by snow,

Icebergs melting on frozen cold land,
Destroying areas of habitation by man,

Is this explanation by global warming,
Or is it the voice of God's warning?

God's warning,
With an unpredictable climate change,
Meteorologists are now considering it strange,

Snowfall in the middle of the spring,
Now that sure is a miraculous thing,

God's warning comes through nature labels,

Rock of my Salvation

If listening, all ears can hear if they're able,

Water has flooded the desert land,
Once was covered by dry hot sand,

Natural disasters are continuing to burst,
Sucking up innocent souls for its thirst,

No man can stop the flaming hot fire,
Covering the town and its entire,

Has global warming hit the earth,
Or has God's warning been disbursed?

Jacqueline James

# If God taps You on the Shoulder...He Shouldn't have to hit, You in the...

If God taps on the shoulder,
He shouldn't have to hit you in the head,

God will tap you on the shoulder, to get your attention,
If you don't get things right, then you weren't listening,

He whispers softly, so you can hear His voice,
If you still mess up, it's by your choice,

God shouldn't have to go upside your head,
With a "stump down", "drag out", just to hear what He said,

When things aren't right on some occasions,
He'll attempt to show you, with a gently persuasion,

But, if you still insist on being disobedient,
You'll be the one who's not succeeding,

# Rock of my Salvation

But, if God directs your path from all that's wrong,
And, let you know you're not alone,

Then change the course from whatever He mentions,
Because, He shouldn't have to hit you in the head, just to
get your attention,

Jacqueline James

# Trust Him...Trust Him...Trust Him...

Trust Him, God sends His miracles through the wind,
To seal your blessings from within,

Opening doors, and changing hearts,
So, keep your faith, while He does His part,

Always trust Him to guide your path,
Throughout generations His words have surpassed,

Trust Him to make your life complete,
Share His love with those you meet,


Trust Him to keep you safe and strong,
Praise His name the whole day long,

Sing to Him a spiritual hymn,
Keep your mind, and thoughts stayed on Him,

# Jesus Fight my Battles...

If you put your trust in the Lord,
If you crash, things will not become hard,

When there's nothing left to say and you have lost your
way,
Jesus will be there to guide you through a difficult day,

Jesus will fight your battles every time,
Just keep your peace and relax your mind,

Jesus will be there as your closest friend,
He is the one in which you can always depend,

When you're facing troubles, Jesus will be with you,
He will never leave nor forsake you, I know this to be true,

When the enemy tries to destroy your soul,
You can count on Jesus to take full control,

When you think no one else cares,
Jesus' love is always going to be there,


Trust in Jesus to fight your battles,
He's the rock of your salvation and everything that matters.

Jacqueline James

# Loving God's Children...

We must love all of God's children when sometimes it's
difficult to do,
The love Jesus has for us will bring us through,

None of us are perfect we all have fallen short from God's
grace,
However, God continues to love us regardless of our
mistakes,

Whenever someone did us wrong, we have held a grudge,
Without showing forgiveness we just criticized then judge,

We have often remained bitter and shown hate toward each
other,
However, our inability to forgive will cause us to struggle,


If we don't forgive nor shall we be forgiven,
Expressing God's love is the fresh start of a new beginning,

Whenever we sincerely show love through our hearts,
Then we have faithfully done our spiritual part,

# Rock of my Salvation

God's love is living, giving, helping, and caring,
Forgiving, considering supporting and sharing,

God wants us to always love each other,
To keep His commandments, we must forgive our sisters
and our brothers.

Jacqueline James

1 John 2,4-5 KJV
He that saith, I know him, and keepeth not his
commandments, is a liar, and the truth is not in him. [5] But
whoso keepeth his word, in him verily is the love of God
perfected, hereby know we that we are in him.

1 John 2,10-11 KJV
He that loveth his brother abideth in the light, and there is
none occasion of stumbling in him. [11] But he that hateth
his brother is in darkness, and walketh in darkness, and
knoweth not whither he goeth, because that darkness hath
blinded his eyes.

Keep God's word by loving on His children,
Don't be blinded by hatred and confusion,

In order to come out of the darkness into God's light,
We must keep His commandments day and night.

# What did God give us?

He gave us all hands to lift with praise,
Along with a heart to worship Him throughout our days,

God gave us a voice to sing His songs,
With other like spirits, so that we're not alone,

God gave us sight to admire the beauty of His land,
With the knowledge to capture His perfect plan,

God gave us compassion to lend to others,
To give a helping hand when they're in trouble,

God gave us legs to walk for many miles,
Along with feet to stand with Him on holy grounds,

God gave us His only begotten son to bring us out,
He came with forgiveness and mercy so we're never
without,

God gave unconditional love for each of us,
With hope through our faith when we trust,

God gave us a mind to worship Him on demand,
With good thoughts to keep His commands,

Jacqueline James


God gave us the promise of eternal life,
By trusting Him completely to guide our lives.

# God's Blessings will Shine...

Just let me tell you about the blessings of the Lord,
Whenever God blesses you, it's because you've worked
hard,

A blessing will come to each of us some day,
All we have to do is trust, believe and pray,

God will send good people to intervene on our behalf,
Who works directly for God as His serving staff,

God wants us to trust Him with our heart and soul,
Then allow His directions to take control,

The world will see that you've been blessed by God,
Through your perfect peace and comforting style,

Your spirit will forever radiate His blessings through love,
That extends to other with compassion and hugs,


Once you separate yourself from the "mind",
Then God's blessing will shine through you every time.

Jacqueline James

"Today's Affirmation"

Today by faith my salvation is promised an eternal life with God. I will walk with God's perfect peace beside me living through my purpose. By God's amazing grace I will defeat any obstacles that attempt to hinder my purpose. I will trust in God's mercy to bring me through my daily challenges. I will honor God daily as I give Him glory in my life. I will humbly accept God as the "Rock of my Salvation"!

I am Prayerful
I am Peaceful
I am Patient
I am Grateful
I am Righteous

Rock of my Salvation

Jacqueline James

Rock of my Salvation

CPSIA information can be obtained
at www.ICGtesting.com
Printed in the USA
LVHW051303170623
750034LV00006B/9